KRISTEN JEWEL

More Than Half-Drowning

A poetry collection

First published by Kristen Jewel 2025

First edition

ISBN (paperback): 979-8-9921323-0-4
ISBN (hardcover): 979-8-9921323-2-8

Illustration by Shelby Ann

This book was professionally typeset on Reedsy.
Find out more at reedsy.com

~

For all the poets and the songwriters whose pretty words just bled right out of them.

~

Contents

III   Part Three: Drowning Love

IV   Part Four: Drowning Self-Esteem

Foreword

I

Part One: Drowning Sadness

More Than Half-Drowning

I think maybe this isn't my first life...
    How else can I explain the overflowing wells of sadness one lifetime
    couldn't possibly be long enough to fill?
I'm over here, digging devastated wells, wondering just how deep can it go?
Digging in trenches, steep ditches, I'm stuck at the bottom of with no hope
of climbing out.

The human body contains 60% water,
    but it's grief I'm more than half-drowning in.

How is that possible?

I am profoundly, profusely, perpetually in pain, and I don't know if it's from
this life's experiences
    or the chemical imbalance in my brain.
    But when it rains, it pours, and baby,
    I'm an eternal, internal, torrential downpour.
    Flash-flooding my own brain
    and treading water is getting harder and harder.

There's a difference between struggling and drowning

And babe,
I'm taking on water like a sinking ship,
Capsize.
And maybe I'm going overboard on the water metaphor,
but now you know what it's like to drown in them too.

Swallowing salt as ocean currents
   pull me down,
   pin me down,
   and crash over me in waves of nonstop sorrow.

I'm hurt.
   And I don't know how to be,
   Or
   How not to be,
   Or
   How to stop,
   Or
   How to resurface.

On the surface... I look fine.
   I'm so fine. I'm just fine. Fine, fine, fine.
   I can't even look people in the eye
   when they ask how I am
   because I know whatever pops out of my mouth will be a lie.
   I'm fine.
   I'm so clearly fine.

I'm just trying to learn how to breathe underwater.

So, I think maybe this isn't my first life.

Because I don't look at the world with wonder,

I wonder
if I look at it like it's underwater
because I've drowned before.
This familiar feeling of lungs burning without air…
I wonder if I drowned and never made it back to shore.
And I keep being reborn
To
drown
and drown
and drown
again
and again.

Until I finally learn how to fucking swim.

Maui

Sometimes, I get so caught up in sadness,
I may as well be attached to a fisherman's hook
because nothing has ever reeled me in so pointedly. Sharply.
A line tugged so tight; tension close to snapping; reinforced specifically to prevent escape.

I'm hooked.

And I don't know if it's because I took the bait or the bait took me,
either way, I can expect to be gutted and filleted,
And maybe I should have fought harder—torn free
no matter what flesh may be ripped from my body.
I don't have gills, but I lose my breath like a fish out of water.

I wish I could change bodies like the demigod Maui in the movie *Moana*.
I could use that hook to change.
No longer dragged in by depression,
I would be set free to soar through skies like seagulls,
swim seas like sharks,
slither like snakes, sliding on soil.

What feeling could ever catch up when you're changing that fast?

I wonder if Maui was running from abandonment
    or if he was just cut free from the line; catch and release: No feast here.
    Just left scarred and hurt. I'm scared of hurt.

Maui. Does it call you too? And no one knows how far it goes?
    Took the Heart of Te Fiti because you couldn't imagine any other way to contribute to life.

I'm sorry.

I'm reeling in feeling after feeling, I reel-ize I've followed the siren-song lure,
    Sure.
    I'm not a demigod, and I can't use a magical hook to change myself.
    But maybe it's not myself I need to change,
    but my perspective.

I am a poet.
    If I can think of
    Words With Weight While Watching Walls, Why Wouldn't Woefulness Willingly Wrought Whimsical Wonder?
    If I can contribute positively to this life with *any* of my words, it would be worth it.

So.
    "Maui, Shapeshifter, Demigod of the Wind and Sea, Hero to All."
    Thank you.
    For helping me realize that "hook" isn't what makes me...
    Me.

Pull Me Down

Pull me down,
    Yes, pull me under
    Pull me, don't push me
Till I drift asunder
thunder may crash
One after another
But if you pull me
Right down under
I'll fall, I'll hide,
From any blunder.
Plunder my depths
But don't leave me aching
Leave me empty
Here for the taking
Yes, take me down
Yes, pull me under
Keep pulling
Keep dragging
Ignore each shudder
Until there's no
Lasting wonder

What happened to her?
They pulled, they grabbed, they dragged…
Pulled me right down under.

Not Breathing

I think the poetry has been knocked from my lungs,,
  Because I can't stop wheezing
    That rasp—it's there—I gasp—for air,
My breath
Freezing.
I used to have so much to say...
But I feel my voice is disappearing.
A vocal erasure I'm not sure I can withstand.

I don't know how many breaths I need to take,
  Before inhalation becomes hyperventilation,
  How many quick successions of breath
  Can keep me living, keep me speaking, keep me breathing.

Some days, I open my mouth, and no sound comes out.
  I haven't lost my voice—my voice has lost me...
  These are the days that make me the saddest.

Pieces

How many pieces of myself
Can I give away?
Till flesh and vein give way,
and bones decay.
How much of myself
Can I give?
How much can I sacrifice?
How much do I really need to live?
Maybe you'd like my life—
Maybe that would finally suffice.

Bobby Pins

If I told you my bobby pins were the only thing holding me together,
would you laugh?
  I have to be honest, they keep me in place.
Though, my bad hair days seem to happen more often than my good hair
days,
  and nothing stays constant.
  I'm constantly redoing it, you know.
  My hair.
  It's not consistent,
  consistently changing,
  I change it as often as tragedy changes me,
  and we all know tragedy is consistency.

So I guess I'm stereotypical that way.
  I also use my hair as a punishment…
  When I feel undeserving, I cut it short
  Cut to the point.

When I read the book *Thirteen Reasons Why* as a teenager,
  I wondered if my hair was to be a symbol of my death.
  They should have known after I'd shown the stereotype.

She cut all of hers off before she offed herself. Was my hair to be the offering for my sacrifice?

But the funny thing about my hair is that it grows so terribly fast.
I try my best not to write about my depression,
repression is the best weapon I have
and I have to use it
so I don't lose this fight.
And maybe that's not the right way to handle how I am—but it's the only way I can.
Repress it.
Suppress it.
Hold it back.

Like my bobby pins hold my hair.

Poetry Notes

If I start writing my suicide notes as poetry,
    does it count as a warning?
    Or is it just the prettiest art?

Each metaphor a jagged cut across
    overstretched blue veins
    turned red by exposure to oxygen.

Each rhyme another dime of blood loss
    over time as the poetry keeps spilling
    from freshly torn wounds.

Each beat reflecting my heartbeat racing
    before slowing,
    metaphor, rhyme, rhythm overflowing.

Just as long as this fucking art
    looks like it's fucking glowing.
    Each bar showing just how far
    my depression is really going.

If time heals all wounds,
    then why am I still waiting?
    Why am I still bleeding?
    Why has this open wound never scabbed over?
    I'm over this feeling.

I stopped making wishes at 11:11 because time has never been on my side.
    They say time is supposed to heal all wounds, but baby,
    I'm still fucking bleeding, the wound is still gaping,
    so you know what,
    I've got beef with the whole motherfucking timeline now.
    Stand back *Marvel*, you aren't the only ones angry that time doesn't work
how we want.

If time won't heal my wounds, I guess I'll stay pleading.
    I guess I'll search for therapy and self-care and anything to stop the bleeding.

And if these poems don't count as notes, I guess I don't know how to leave
my goodbyes.
    I could always just stay, of course.
    But if they do count,
    I'll save them in volumes and texts and tomes and keep my goodbyes bound
in metaphors.
    Because I don't *want* to say goodbye. Not really. Not Voluntarily.
    Instead, I'll keep these feelings poetic. Artistic.
    I'll just keep writing my bleeding heart as the prettiest art.

Little Deaths

How many little deaths can I die
until I stop coming back to life?
Raised like the dead
Not dead,
but half alive;
A zombie in my own life.
Raised from a grave
I'd rather be at peace in.
Tucked away under churned soil,
buried like every emotion I stuff down
Deep within my heart's soft ground.

Kill Me

Kill me.
>My body is entirely breakable,
>you'll see.
My soul entirely shakable,
why wouldn't it be?
How couldn't it be?
Empathy attacking me,
popping like grease from a pan,
it burns me.
Tiny explosions of boiling agony
everywhere.

So, kill me.
>Don't make me feel
>when I'd rather embrace being numb,
>because feeling how much I feel,
>is so fucking dumb.

I wish apathy consumed me,
>because feeling nothing
>is so much easier than feeling everything.

I can see why people turn themselves off from this world.
  Lose humanity,
  bit by bit,
  because it's too hard to feel all of it.

Yeah.
  Kill me.

A teacher once told me there's more than one way to kill a person.
  More than one type of death.
  You don't have to die outside to die inside
  and I think I'm dying a little each day.

Metaphor aside,
  there's just no way to live through—
  and yes—this hurts my pride,
  but I've lost count of just how many times I've cried.
  How many times I've pried
  feeling after feeling
  from aching, empty cavern hearts.
  I want to be hollow.
  I swallow each bitter breath,
  hoping feelings start easing,
  but each bitter breath is another bitter death.

So, kill me.
  Or can you not kill what's already dead?

This Grave of a Body

I n this grave of a body,
    I've certainly buried my soul
    dug a hole
rusted shovels scraping,
threw myself in whole.

Put a smile here, put a frown there,
    but don't ever appear like you don't care.
    Put on a mask; make your personality disappear.

I've killed myself so many times, this grave's in disrepair.
    This grave is a place of mourning,
    you can see that in my eyes,
    you can see my haunted warning,
    you can see this face is a disguise.

I've adorned the grave with makeup,
    god forbid a place of rest isn't made up.
    In this grave of a body, my soul is not at peace.
    You just see a piece of me begging for release.

And in this grave of a body,
    you can see the corpse is turning cold,
    sulfur burning, blood is clotting;
    I think something here is rotting.

Haunted Memories

Memories
Don't haunt me, please.
Ghosts I can't appease,
My fragile mind won't ease,
Bitter Nostalgic tease.
These mindless decrees
Can't escape my histories
Muddied with sleaze.
I'm in fight or flight "freeze"
Heart racing like a maelstrom breeze.
Please. Memories. Stop haunting my fantasies.

I Miss You

W hat I have learned from death
is that you never stop missing the departed.
You don't move on,
or get "over" their passing.

You just get used to missing them.

You get used to the feeling of pain.
  What was once raw and new,
  I didn't know how to handle.
  But as time went on, I got used to how it felt.
  Like wearing rings for the first time,
  uncomfortable between the knuckles until you've worn them for years.
  Until you feel naked when you're not wearing them.
  You learn to get used to the feeling.
  In fact, you depend on it.
  Like the arthritis in my spine,
  it's a physical, bone-deep ache I've accepted I'll always have.
  And that's how I see death.
  I'll never stop missing you. I still miss you.
  Your absence will never stop hurting me.

I'll keep missing you, and it will keep hurting me until I'm gone, too.

On My Knees Begging to Repent

I haven't spent
   much time on my knees,
   begging to repent;
relentless sins clawing at my mind.

I don't think I'm a kind person.
  I mean, I try.
  But I make a lot of mistakes.
  And I guess that's all it takes
  in my mind. In my eyes.
  I despise myself.

I'm not allowed the grace I'd give another person,
  because I'm supposed to be perfection.
  No, I am not perfect,
  but I keep holding myself to perfect standards
  that I know I'll never meet.

I'm supposed to be perfect to other people.
  With grace and kindness,
  but I don't find this.

I think I hurt people when I don't mean to,
    haven't meant to,
    but caused pain all the same, and I'm the one to blame.
    I'm sorry that I make such big mistakes.

And I'm sorry I haven't spent days and weeks on my knees,
    weak in the knees,
    desperate pleas for forgiveness
    spilling from my lips.

I know I should be kneeling,
    but I can't help but feeling
    like I don't deserve the forgiveness.
    Like even asking for it is too much.
    Too presumptuous.

And maybe that's where I fall short.
    Maybe I should be on my knees
    for apologies.
    Not seeking forgiveness,
    just expressing sorrow.
    And trying to be better for tomorrow.
    Instead of living in the past,
    trying to redeem my future.
    Not for me.
    But because I don't want to hurt the people around me.

I really, truly, desperately,
    don't want to hurt the people around me.

Scream

I want to run atop a hill
    Where I will scream;
    scream for so much.
I'll scream for every broken dream,
I'll stand and scream despite the chill.

And then I'll scream for every dream come true,
    I'll scream until I don't know what to do.
    I'll scream for the sad, and I'll scream for the happy,
    I will scream until my face is blue.

I am screaming for everything that's real.
    I scream... for everything I feel.

Terrible Poetry

I think your poetry is terrible.
Incomparable, unshareable, unbearable.
Like whispered secrets meant for the dying, not long before last breath, they're gone.

Don't get me wrong.
I'm not trying to tear you down, it's just with every word, you make me drown.
I see before my eyes what you've gone through,
And I don't want to,

But dreamlike, I'm seeing through molasses-colored glasses
Your stories are too real, and just, damn the things you make me feel. It's too surreal.

How terrible the path you've walked to roll stones from your tongue.
Heavy words don't come from light experiences.
But it breaks my heart what heartbreaks make aesthetically pleasing poetry.

Does your glass-shard-embedded heart prick you deeper with each contracting beat?

I know mine does.

So, I think your poetry is terrible.

Terribly powerful.
  Terribly heart-wrenching.
  Terribly painful.
  Terribly sad.

Terrible.

Split

Weary pain; endured.
Strain; suffered.
Yet urges my heart
Free from dread.
Aching, echoing scream
Stabs the Heart.
My spirit soars
Heart's desire… or anguish of spirit?

You asked me to Stay

Y ou asked me to Stay.
    But…
    I don't think you understand how badly I've wanted to go.
Leave.
Finally find reprieve from this life,
because I don't believe things get better.
Relieve my pain in the most permanent way,
because there's no way things can be good one day.

You asked me to Stay,
    but I don't think you understand how much I've wanted to go,
    disappear,
        give in to all the disparate fear.
    Leaving this life has never been a plan in motion more than a following
emotion.
    The desire not to exist exists in my body, my being, screaming of fleeing.

You asked me to Stay,
    be the Reason you no longer feel like a stray,
    wandering, alone, lonely, and astray.

You asked me to Stay by your side
    and I think if it had been only words, I'd have let myself slide.
    After all, who would have cared if I died?
    But then I found music. I found songs; I found melodies.
    I found reasons to keep listening, to keep singing, open to possibilities.

People tell you that your music saved their lives,
    and I'm here to confirm your music has kept me alive.
    It's not the only reason I Stay, but it sure is a monumental one, anyway.
    You say it saved your lives too, and I'm thinking that's probably true.

I don't think you understand how much I wanted to go.
    And I hope you know,
    you have every right to claim the light you spread.
    To influence thousands, if not millions, to Stay.
    Your joy sparks so much joy, chasing away the gray.

You asked me to Stay, and
    you made me feel like everything might be okay.
    Maybe not today, maybe not tomorrow,
    but day by day,
    you are chasing away my sorrow.

Sure, you asked me to Stay,
    and damn if you didn't show me how to.
    In every word
    every gesture, every deed,
    every lyric, every beat,
    every song, every street
    you've walked so long, so strong, so far.

You've shown me what Staying really looks like, even when it's hard.

Maybe it's silly.
  Thinking a band or music or lyrics can save your life.
  But you've made me feel like part of something
  instead of nothing. And finding something, anything, that can bring you
just a little bit of joy is worth holding on for,
  worth keeping, worth fighting for.

Worth Staying for.
  Worth waiting around for more.
  Because if I leave… I can't see them anymore.
  And that…
  Seems worth sticking around for.

You asked me to Stay.
  And for one of the first times in my life… I want to.
  And though I need you infinitely more than you need me,
  I beg; please: ask me to Stay.

If you ask me to Stay,
  maybe, I can…
  I can… Maybe, I—I can; Can I?
  I… I… I will.
  I definitely, definitively will.
  I will
  Stay.

II

Part Two: Drowning Rage

Shedding Skin

S hedding skin
    Shredding sin
      Breaking myself open.
Ripping flesh from muscle,
Tearing away my exterior,
No longer smooth and supple
Exposing my interior.

If I'm a skinless, bloody mass
    Do you think you'll finally see me?
    A horrific skinned nightmare
    My insides breaking free.
    You could no longer treat me invisibly…

Couldn't act like you didn't see, wouldn't see, never saw

When I wear it oh so freely.
    Shedding all my skin, every crack and flaw,
      wearing all my pain outside, exposed and bloody raw.

Fire and Ash

There are days I feel like fire, and then there are days I feel like ashes.

    On the days I feel like ashes, even the gentlest breeze could send me drifting,
spread me thin, dissipate my very being
scattered through the air.
One little wind is all it would take to blow me away.

On the days I feel like fire, I burn to the center of my core.
    I ignite thoughts and change; I am capable of destroying forests.
    Not even the rain can tame my flame; when the wind blows, I rage.
    Red, all red, lust-filled for everything to feel my hate.
    Knowledge of: When we all burn, then we can restart and rebuild.
    Hope for more comes through my blaze.

There are days I feel like fire, and there are days I feel like ashes.
    Light a match, strike my phosphorus, watch me burn myself and the world
to the ground.
    Some days I'm fire, some days I'm ash.

Fire and ash are my main elements.

Fuck with me, and you'll feel my pain.

Rooted and crawling inferno, ready to open and swallow my enemies in the name of the lord.

Don't sin; don't confuse me, my mind is a firestorm.

Ready to eat up all the conformed humans that live life in petty ways.

Some days, I'm fire, and you'll see my flame.

Other days, I'm ashes, and I'm flowing with the wind,

ready to ignite if things don't go my way.

If you feel the audacity,
    strike me
    and find out just which one I feel like today.

~This is a collaboration poem written with the Poet Doraly.

Burning Poems

How to burn a poem as you write it: A Guide.
How to burn your poem:
Put the pencil to page, and start writing.
Let out all of the inner turmoil, let out all of your rage.
Let the words you scribble act as sage,
let them smoke out the demons.
Evil spirits, begone with every stanza, line, and song.
Write faster.
Let the graphite against paper create so much friction and
the bars you scribe burn so hot they cause affliction.
If you want to burn your poem as you write it,
you have to let your words burn; you have to let the pages turn,
like churning butter, you work them over and over
set them ablaze, work out the flame.
You can't let go of rage until you name it in words.
The words you pen, they must be scalding.
It's the only way you can get them out.
Burning like sulfur, the demons leave your mind,
leaving nothing but inked words behind.
This is how you burn your poem as you write it
leaving nothing but smoking cinder letters to find.

Like soot and ash, they may smudge the writing.
But if you've burned your poem just right,
those charred and burned scarred pages will be such a brilliant sight.

Anger's Name

I asked Anger to tell me her real name,
    but she scoffed and flipped me off.
    Flipped me the middle finger, refused to linger.
She's tough, but I think I can crack her.
I think I can get her to stay,
get her to say
what her name is.

I asked Anger to tell me her real name,
    but she shamed me instead.
    Told me to mind my business. Watch where I tread.

I asked again, and I think she got mad…
    She punched a wall, broke her hand,
    but when she cried… I could swear she was sad.

I guess I should change my strategy,
    maybe be less direct.
    But no matter how softly I spoke, how gently I tip-toed,
    her face went scarlet, and she told me I have no respect.
    No matter how many coats of sugar I used,

her tongue still left me bruised.

Exasperated, I asked her again,

"Anger, what is your real name? Please give me a hint."

She squinted at me and said, "I'll give you a hint if you tell me yours."

I spoke my name and asked that she do the same.

Anger glared, and I thought she'd make another deflection, another rejection,

but she answered:

"Of course. My name is yours," said my reflection.

Anger is Easier Than Sadness

A nger... Is easier than sadness, but harder to hold onto—
and

oh.

How I've held you.

Like a fistful of sand, and
  it's Slipping through my fingers like I never had a grasp—
  Slipping through my fingers so fast—
  Slipping through my fingers like I can't get a grip—

You can't rip this from me.

With clenched fists, I hold on tight,
  With clenched fists, I still fight,
  With clenched fists, nails digging into palms; knuckles turning white,

This is my death grip.

But... my hands are shaking. I am shaken.

How can I hold on to anger when it so desperately wants to leave?
You were supposed to be there for me. Not make me have to leave,

Because your anger was easier for you to clutch in your fingers—your crutch—
and your anger lingers because anger is easier than sadness.

But isn't it so much fucking harder to hold on to?

And I—I don't want to be like you.

So, I'm slowly learning how to let go... brushing beachfuls of fury from
sweat-slicked palms.
    Death-grip loosening, fingers unfurling,
    And I can only hope that yours are uncurling too.
    Because I see your hands shaking—I see you shaken.

And I am so... Sad for you.

And sadness... that is the hardest fucking thing to get through.

Unallowed Anger

I 'm not allowed my anger.
   I've never been allowed my anger.
   And I think it's something I've struggled with for a long time,
   like the lid of a jar screwed on too tight, but instead of turning left you're
turning right,
   jamming the problem completely.

I think it's funny I'm never allowed to be angry.
   When I get mad, everyone around me seems to be mad that I'm mad…
   No validation of my feelings to be had.

And once or twice is whatever, but this is whenever I feel valid anger.

Why can't I express my emotions in a healthy way?

I'm not punching walls.
   I'm not whipping children with belts.
   I'm not hitting 5-year-olds with dress shoes.
   I'm not pinching skin, pulling hair, or spitting shaking rage into faces.

I'm breaking the cycle.

I would never let my anger be violent.
What happened to me only made me more angry,
but I'm not allowed to talk about it, have to bottle it in that jar.

Bottle it. Bottle all of this fucking anger inside, twist the lid harder.

I'm bottling anger like genies,
   but instead of giving wishes,
   I'm giving vicious,
   my anger only growing into something malicious,
   making me want to punch walls, too.

Bite myself when the anger is too much.
   Hurt myself instead of the people around me,
   sinking teeth into already bruised flesh,
   because who the fuck cares if I'm hurt just a little more?

No, I'm not allowed my anger.
   So, I guess I'll keep writing poetry instead of healing furious thoughts inside
my head.

I don't have violent bones in my body,
   but I have violence in my mind.
   Anger still clinging in tiny grains,
   like shrapnel from long-exploded bombs,
   the impact long gone, long dead,
   the aftermath still sticking in the explosion's stead.
   The carnage so widespread, nothing could measure.
   I guess even a sealed jar can shatter under too much pressure.

Holding Back

I 'm holding back.
    Constantly.
    Consistently.
Biting my tongue,
clenching my teeth,
holding my breath in each lung.

I think I could explode
    from just how much I hold back.
    Under attack from what wants to break free,
    but I don't think I'll ever be
    free enough to be me.

I have to hold back.
    Better to appear like I lack,
    like I'm lacking,
    hold back, all inside, keep stacking
    pile after pile
    mile after mile
    until my blood turns vile.
    Until I'm spitting bile

in overflowing style.
Keep holding back.
Pack everything in.
Maybe I'll contain so much
I could even implode.

Pretty Rages

Pretty words
For pretty pages
Pretty words
For pretty cages
Lock me up
For many ages
Till the world
Forgets my face and
Till I forget
My own place and
Pretty bars lock away
Pretty rages
Look away, yes
She's contagious

Sorry Conspiracy

Y ou are sorry: A conspiracy theory.
    Because theory is all I've got
    and I think you just forgot
I have eyes in addition to ears.
Here's the conspiracy:
You say you're sorry, sorries are all I hear,
but I see you too. I see what you do.
And don't do.
I can see you repeat the same action
echo pain
again
and again
and again.

Your haunted echoes of hollow words
    reverberate like stampeding herds,
    quaking the ground with false resound,
    resounding slap-sorries are just empty gestures,
    shaking every sorry I've found.
    Empty promises when you keep the action despite the lectures.

I can't keep begging you not to hurt me,
    just for you to nod, agree, say sorry, wash, rinse, repeat hurting me.

The conspiracy is that you're never sorry.
    Not when every motion your body makes contradicts the words from your lips.

The theory is that your "I'm sorry"
    really translates to:

Nothing.

There's no metaphor in translating your apology.

Because your empty, hollow, meaningless words are dead to me.

Apology Tour

The funniest part of your apology tour
was the insincerity.
Getting mad at people
who no longer want to hear the tombstones of dead words
housed in your graveyard tongue
is actual insanity.
It is not a shortcoming of the wronged to refuse to acknowledge ghosts.
It is not the fault of the wounded to refuse being haunted.
If the axe apologizes to the tree,
I don't think the tree wants to hear the apology.
You sever a limb on a whim
and think simple sorries guarantee your absolution?
The tree is already cut down,
is splintered,
and I don't blame them for not wanting to hear from the axe.
How many dead branches have you collected?
How much kindling have you prepared for the fire?
Some actions are beyond apology.
The tree doesn't have to forgive the axe,
and I think deep down,
you know that's true.

Be so for real right now.
It's gaslighting 101 to turn your shitty deeds into the fault of the victim.
Victim blaming, while widely accepted in this 2025 society,
is not, has never been, and will never be cool.
Get your firewood somewhere else, you blunted axe.

Cuntestant

S omeone once told me,
"I hate seeing you succeed when I'm not succeeding."

And biiiiitch.
I just have to ask:
When in the fuck did you ever think I was competing?
If you compete with your friends,
that's just a beginning to many, many ends.
There was never a competition to me.

I may compete with my anxiety,
I may compete with my depression,
but what would ever give you the impression
that I'm competing with *you*?
That's something I just don't do; won't do.

So let me get mean for a second.

You traded friendship for a one-sided rivalry,
never to be returned.
Want to ride in on your white horse, like the heroic cavalry,

but comfortable with bridges burned.
You wanna spit bars,
show that you make the bread,
but you've set the bar so low,
you're trippin' on em instead.

If Kendrick is the biggest hater,
 I'll gladly settle for silver
 because I'm still medals ahead.
 Up in the lead, up front,
 when all you have is A front.
 Sorry, am I being too blunt?
 I know you can't handle the brunt
 because you're just a cun—testant.
 Contestant.
 In your own imaginary competition in your head.
 Because I was never competing
 with someone not worth defeating,
 an embarrassment to be seen beating.

Poison Words

Whoever said sticks and stones are the ones breaking your bones,
sure as fuck never met you.
Because all your words do
are wreck me;
twist the knife in my belly.
I've never known more strife
than the hatred poison you spew.
Words can never hurt you?
Right.
They'll only fucking kill you.

Emotions in Ombré

I think the weirdest part of accepting how angry I am
is realizing how closely related it is to how sad I am.
In my mind, they're such separate emotions.
Like water and oil,
they shouldn't mix.
One can float on top of the other,
but they're physically incapable of blending.
Why are they so capable of blending?
Like ombré, they bleed so seamlessly into each other.
An art palette of my insides splashed across a canvas
to paint a bigger picture.
When art critics say they like the dimensions,
I guess I didn't realize how metaphorical that could be.
When they ask what the art is saying,
I didn't realize maybe I was trying to say something, too.
If my anger and sadness just *have* to hold hands,
I guess I'm glad they're trying to say something.
Even if I don't always understand.
But I guess that's art.
Not everyone understands it.
Not even the artist.

III

Part Three: Drowning Love

"Sometimes" Love

You say you love me... "Sometimes."
But I need you to know,
I need you to hear me,
even when you're not near me,
I love you at all times.
Not "Sometimes."
Even when my heart is breaking after taking pain after pain,
I love you All Times.

But I guess... I should never have wished for reciprocation.
You can't love me All Times.

I guess I'll take "Sometimes" love.
I guess, it must be better than No love.
"Sometimes" love... hurts more than I thought it would,
more than I thought it should,
could I be the one who's broken?
Am I so needy, so greedy, that "Sometimes" love isn't enough love?
That "Sometimes" love kind of feels the same way No love does?
I guess... I just thought that unconditional love meant... without condition.

I don't want to beg you to love me.
　I shouldn't have to beg you to love me.

Don't leave me pleading
　leave me bleeding.
　my heart out on my sleeve and
　leaking blood every time another person turns to leave.
　Leaving me to believe
　I am unlovable.
　I am only lovable in small doses,
　small quantities,
　just "Sometimes."

One supposes,
　a little love could potentially go a long way,
　but is there really just no way for you to love me always?
　I hear "always" in movies and "always" always moves me,
　and if other people can have so much love in their hearts
　Why can't you?
　What is it about me that your "always" love just can't do?

Do I settle for "Sometimes?"
　Even if "Sometimes" love makes me feel like my heart is being torn open
with blunt fingernails and butter knives and rusted chisels.
　I don't understand how your "Sometimes" love can be so callous,
　or if your heart is only full of roughened callouses.
　But why does your blunt ripping ache so much worse than a sharpened
knife?
　Why does the dull blade hurt so much worse than a sharp one?
　Can't you cut me off any cleaner?
　Can't you kill me off any neater?

"Sometimes" love can be so rough,

"Sometimes" love can be so tough,
"Sometimes" love is… not enough.

I guess I just have to come to terms with the fact that I am a "Sometimes" love.
    And I think I'd better learn to be okay with that.
    Take the blow.
    Take the hit.
    Even if sometimes… your "Sometimes" love is not worth it.

Love Language Barrier

I f touch is a love language,
   then I've hit a language barrier.

   Too foreign to be fluent in the native tongue.
   When I crossed the distant seas,
   skinship sailed without me,
   leaving me adrift;
   Overboard.
   On an island, alone,
   touch-starved on a faraway shore.
   I've never known such desolate hunger digging into the deepest part of my
core.
   I'm stranded;
   Surrounded by sand, and
   touched only by sunlight and moonlight and starlight.
   And it's my own fault. It's this vessel's fault; that ship has sailed.

If touch is a love language, then,
   I've hit a love barrier.

A border between me and the rest of the world.

Touch hungry behind a wall of my own building,
desperate hunger clawing for affection, but my body pulling me in a different direction, deflection of all intention to touch.,
A physical protection of feeling too much.
I honestly don't know what's wrong with me.
What leads me to crave touch at the same time fearing it?

I've never been fluent in love language, always speaking a different tongue than everyone around me, surround me with

Touch. It's human nature to touch;
It's tough.
We crave skin-to-skin
too much.
Hand in hand,
shoulder to shoulder,
cry on mine, lean on mine, rest on mine.
Though, mine may feel colder.
I don't know how
and I don't know when,
I became terrified to touch.
Too uncomfortable in my own skin.
Stiff and heartless like tin,
body tense.
Awkward.
Hesitant.
Like I need oil to unlock
each of my rusted joints just to create any sort of movement,
a moment, and it's tragic.

Because touch is one of my love languages.
And I've cut myself off.
I've forgotten how to speak it. How to feel it.

I don't think the Tin Man was ever lacking a heart, just human connection.
A body in motion stays in motion,
and a body untouched stays broken. Frozen.

If touch is a love language,
　　then I've hit a language barrier.
　　I've hit a love barrier.
　　I've hit a love language barrier.

And I so badly want to learn the language.
　　Become fluent.
　　Until love flowers from my fingers like second nature.

Exorbitant Sincerity

D o you know how to love without money?
How to show care?
How to share feeling.
How to learn love language without dealing?
You can't buy hearts,
You can't buy love,
You can't throw money at every problem above.
Feelings don't have a price,
Not going once, twice, thrice,
Auctioning off affection to the highest bidder.
Money obsession
Leaves me bitter
Greed infection
Not a gambling quitter
I need you to hear this lesson
Let this be your hardest hitter.
Do you even know how to love without throwing money like you're owed?
Treating love like something you've owned.
You can't buy me,
Though my love is free,
Sad that even the wealthiest in the world

Can't afford that fee.
I guess it's too expensive
To just love someone with sincerity.

You Can't Taste Love

F irst step into sunlight reminds me of the heat…
we never had.
Second step into the powdered snow makes me remember frigid.
Because frigid is a brrr word—Stop.
Frigid is a brrr word—Stop.

Boots buried in frost; I stop to stare at the light reflecting from the snow hill.
I gather a bit of the light into the crooks of my fingers,
and tilting my head to see better… I see:

What we had was a frost-covered heart carved into the form of this hill.
And if I could taste love, it would be in this tiny pale powder I hold in my hand.
If I could taste love,

it would not seep through my fingers to fall toward a hard ground.

If I could taste love, it would not dissipate on the tip of my tongue like the word itself.

But you can't… taste love.

Snow turns hard in your mouth before it dissolves.
If the words are like stone in your mouth…
Let them dissolve.
Take the time to swallow that fluid truth.
Remember the taste on your lips of that icy kiss,
Remember that taste: Because you can't taste love.

Ghostly Scars

The ghost of scars you left still linger, littered across my heart.
And it's not that you broke it,
No.
It's that you sliced into it with a steak knife of serrated insults
Cutting ragged, jagged, jaded gaping wounds into the too-sensitive muscle
Leaving holes where once was whole.
And it's not that I loved you.
I knew I didn't.
But that never made me impervious to put-downs.
Let downs.

And man, you really let me down.

So, the wounds healed over,
Leaving ghostly white shimmer stripes
Haunting my heart with scars I can't even see.
Scarring me with the ghost of your apathy.

Love Me

"Love me!"

This is what I call to my cat when she refuses to cuddle me.

You can bet, much like any feline, she will let you know when she is ready to be pet.

"Love me!"

This is what I yell at my friends when I just need attention… they reassure me that they do indeed love me. And I know this is needy, but in attention, I am entirely greedy.

Love me.

This is what I think to every person who has ever hated or felt indifferent to me, indifferently, impartially, for some reason, I feel compelled to keep killing myself to get to the graveyard party, keep changing myself.

Maybe, if I cut off enough pieces, I'll fit into a smaller box
because your indifference is a coffin; bury me deep.
I keep killing myself for people I don't even like,
specifically because they don't like me,
and that's like,
fucking crazy.

"Love me."

This is what I write on a sticky note placed eye-level on my mirror. And I wish… I wish that girl's eyes would linger longer.

I wish she would listen,

and not to a society who tells her to hate herself every day.

After all, I know she makes it a point never to ask anyone to do anything she wouldn't.

"Love me."

A response to the song "A Thousand Years" by Christina Perri

You have died
every day
waiting for me.
Darling,
I'm afraid I have died
every day
waiting for me, too.
You have waited for a thousand years,
and I wonder...
Can you really, truly, faithfully
wait a thousand more?

Open For Use

I have an "Open For Use" sign carved into the skin of my forehead and,
No matter how many times I try to stitch that shit together, it keeps
ripping open at the seams—
Seems like my bleeding heart is bleeding through these seams for everyone
to see.

Please use me.
Obviously, I welcome it with open arms. Take advantage.
They're open for you to fill and ravage, slice open.
Just call me your 1 a.m. emotional booty call; after all, I'm always here, and
you know I'll always answer.

So, text me that you're bored.

Oh, and forgive the use of my ambiguous "you," but so many have had the
ambiguous use of me that I can't keep track anymore.

I'm only here for entertainment.

So, why don't you rub salt into the gashes in my forehead and the tears down
my arms; just to watch the blood run out.

To remind me, I'm supposed to be open 24/7,
Forget stitching. Throw away that needle and thread.

I've got blood-stained white threads stitched halfway through my open wounds,
    hanging uncut out of my half-held-together skin
    because you tugged at the ends
    and I'm half-unraveled.
    Only began stitching the gaping holes in my arms
    when you decided I looked better half-open,
    so strum these loose guitar strings to the tune of your own song,
    they only sing for you.

And I want to cut these ends,
    so I don't have any loose ones,
    but you stole the knife meant to cut me free and stabbed me in the back instead,
        I said I was bleeding out, so you pulled it out and let the red run rampant,
        and my bleeding heart said YES.

Because you pulled at those blood-stained white puppet thread strings,
    pulling them tight to my skin,
    pulling my arms open so you could come in every time I tried to say no.

So open, arms!
    Open arms.
    Gaping open, open arms, open for use, your marionette torn open,
    gracefully spilling scarlet,
    dyeing my bonds prettier for you to control.

As I start getting dizzy from lack of blood and gasp for lacking air,
    you throw the needle and knife and thread at my feet
    before I fall to my knees… and you walk away.

Please use me?

I still have life flowing through these wounds,
    but my vision goes dark,
    and I wonder if you were the tourniquet to my still-bleeding heart,
    only I've lost so much blood I can't see straight anymore,
    so I fumble for more thread and a needle I can no longer see
    and realize...

I will die.
    Before I get any more puppet thread in me.
    And I'm glad.
    Because I can't bleed for you anymore.

Any of you.

And it hurts.
    It really, really hurts.
    But I have nothing left to give.
    I have nothing left to give.

Blood-Red Roses

Is the red on my roses love or blood?

Roses are red
Violence is too,
How can I know
If my love rings true?

When love and blood
Bleed the same color,
How can I differ
One from another?

Maybe it's not so cut and dry
When push comes to shove,
Maybe it's one and the same
I'm just bleeding love.

So, I'll paint your pretty roses
With all the love and blood my heart can shed,
With all my aching pain and longing,
Until all the roses in your garden

are painted deep blood-red.

Can't Stay Away

There's something about you
  that pulls me in, draws me in,
  something I'll fight,
but I know I won't win.
You pull me in deeper,
push me, pull me, every night and day.
Because there's just no way
I could stay away.
I can't leave you be,
my mind has no say.
My body is talking for me;
You match my crazy, okay?
With your lack of control
I might struggle to break free,
but as the writhing takes its toll,
I close my eyes so I can't see.
Take a breath, but I can't breathe.
Hold me tightly, bind me down,
trap me in your chains of sound.
In the darkness, there's something to be said
of blindfolds and shadows and lights made of red.

I need you here; I need you now,

Stay by my side, inside, drop the mic, take a bow, bow down, I plea, yes sir, yes, please.

You are My Bias

You are my bias,
    and by this,
      I mean:
I can't imagine a world without you in it. I couldn't survive.

You are my bias,
    and by this,
    I mean:
Thank you so much for just being alive.

You are my bias,
    and by this,
    I mean:
You are everything I've ever wanted to be.
Everything I've ever admired, you inspired me.
Inspire me, I aspire to be
more like you; less like me.

You are my bias,
    and by this,
    I mean:

I can't believe you don't see in you
what I do.

I can't comprehend
    that you could possibly have a single negative thought about yourself in
your head
    when all I think of when I think of you
    is love and positivity.
    You are the world to me.
    My bias, I'm biased to love you implicitly.

Intentional Love

I think I take you for granted...
   granted,
   I don't mean to.
Like you're my next lungful of air
I need you to live
but I'm not thinking about every inhale
exhale,
I'm just breathing.
like a reflex.
Like you're not the very oxygen keeping me alive.
I just got too comfortable,
knowing my body will keep breathing
whether I think about it or not.
I keep loving you
like a reflex
whether I think about it or not,
and I think I should think about it more intentionally.
I love you more than I can ever say, written or verbally, but

I want to love you loudly, even though my voice is quiet.
   I want to love you loudly, even if my shyness won't allow it.

I can love you in every action, even if my voice won't speak it.
I can love you in every touch, even when my words up and quit.

Let me love you loudly, quietly.
Because sometimes my words just don't hit.

I used to be so scared to say, "I love you."
Maybe because I was taught a love that hurts.
But when you loved me so softly, so gently… that was a first.

You're the bee's knees,
and I'll work harder to tell you every day.
Work harder not to take you for granted,
to think about my love in a more intentional way.

Because

You've loved me in every action, but your voice definitely shouted it.
You've loved me in every touch, and I don't think your words have ever quit.
You've given me a better standard of what love should be,
and you've shown that you still hear my love, even when I'm quiet.

So, even if my love's a reflex, I'll never take you for granted;
treasure each lungful of air that I breathe.
I'll treasure you like oxygen, like a balm of a full breath, my lung's relief;
you're my relieve.

My Furnace

I know I joke about you being my furnace,
   but your warmth is the furthest thing from a joke.
   Warm from the inside out,
the heat you radiate like the radiant sun warms me from the outside in,
your warmth, blankets to my skin,
your warmth, mittens to my heart,
your warmth, balm to my soul.
When I say you are warm, sure, I mean physically.
But I also mean metaphorically.
It's your warm personality, personally,
I see the warmth in the way you care for me so carefully.
You tuck me into the bed of your warmth,
surround me with the softest blankets,
make sure not an inch of skin is exposed to cold.
Like a nest of your warmth I could live in,
the warmth you share is really something to behold.

IV

Part Four: Drowning Self-Esteem

Inadequately Me

There's a piece inside of me
  that's always wanted to be taken away,
  taken to a far and fanciful place,
a magical kingdom,
so far away from my life.
It's not the people around me,
it's this life's circumstances that have me crazy.
No questioning why I want to go so badly,
or that will only invite the guilt in.
How can I say how badly I want to be swept away
when I'm supposed to be content?
Supposed to love my life, anyway.
Any day
I'll leave this place.
Do what I want to do,
live how I want to live.
I have a friend who asks me
what's stopping me from living the life I want right now?
Maybe it's not the place I'm in... Physically or metaphorically.
Maybe it's me.
Probably it's me.

Maybe I'm the one holding myself back
though I can't explain why.
No pattern I can track,
no proper explanation, nothing,
and I have an answer for everything
to my own detriment.
Maybe it's not my surroundings,
not my environment,
but me.
My own brain.
My own inadequacy.
Inadequately... me.

Mountains of Anxiety

A nxiety says, "Don't open your mouth."
Anxiety wonders: If you keep your mouth shut long enough, will your lips seal themselves like caverns on mountain faces?
A rock-slide, lock-jaw closure.
If you stop talking long enough, maybe you'll forget how, just like the mountain did.

Anxiety says everyone looking at you wishes you would shut up because you don't have anything important to say—says you can't touch lives because mountains don't have hands or voices, only open mouths screaming in silence.
Anxiety asks why you write poetry...
You're not sure, you only know you were putting on makeup in the bathroom when electricity shocked your system, and you had to get this out on paper before a thought avalanche buried it.

Anxiety says you should write about ALL issues, but not issues that don't belong to you because that's rude, but so is being exclusive, and you can't just keep writing about how sad you are, but

Anxiety holds hands with depression—they're besties, buying each other brunch to keep feeding into each other over mimosas.

But anxiety doesn't want this to be about depression—Anxiety is very mean, and you try to tune it out, but it's in your head, and how do you tune out your head?

You're trying to put anxiety outside of yourself, but anxiety says you're confused and don't know which thoughts are yours and which are anxiety's, and that's GOOD.

But you try anyway. Try to name it, something like "cheating ex who always put you down" because that makes it tangible—challengeable.

Anxiety begs you to stop speaking and fall through the floor, but you don't.

Because your feet are the base of this mountain, your body the heart, your mouth a cavern, and mountains are KNOWN for standing strong, so you will too.

Wind can cut them, rain feels like bullets, they may erode, crumble, or slide—but it takes an awful lot of shit to take down a mother fucking mountain, and nothing short of a fault will move you from this spot.

And you haven't yet forgotten how to speak.

Wearing Serenity

My entire life, I've worn anxiety on my sleeve
Leaving no room for hearts.

Anxiety makes up both sleeves,
covering up both arms.

I hate wearing anxiety,
I hate that it's inside of me,
My god, I'd so much rather be,
Wearing nothing but serenity.

To have a cloak of calm,
A sweater of peace,
A cardigan of unbothered fleece
An untroubled balm of a sleeve.

Instead of wearing my anxiety
I'd be so much more at peace
Sparing me my dignity
Spending eternity in fuzzy tranquility

Wearing serenity.

Awkward

I don't want to be here.
 Or there.
 Or anywhere, really.
Fight with my own self-consciousness,
own stiffened awkwardness,
why can't I be aware of myself less?
Why can't I just be natural in my own skin?
My own body.
I carry embarrassment as extra weight,
weighed down by my awareness,
I wish I was oblivious.
I wish I had the gift of effortlessness.
Effortless charm.
Effortless speaking.
Effortless standing.
Effortless being.
Instead of being conscious of my every move,
every twitch,
someone, please switch
bodies with me.
Either take me away or take the awkward from my soul.

Don't make me sit with this.
Because it's really growing old.

Broken Things

If broken things could talk,
   I think I'd be a little louder.
   If broken things could talk,
My voice wouldn't blend like setting powder.
If broken things could talk,
I wouldn't be so set on paper and pen
I wouldn't be so much better in ink
distinct voice might be heard then.
But this is a game of "if."
And sadly, broken things can't talk.
My body can walk
Jump
Climb
Run
But speaking has been my biggest uphill battle
A battle I've more lost than won.
Told I'm too quiet, soft-spoken, good enough to place,
But never number one.
If broken things could talk,
Man,
I think I'd like to hear my voice.

Make a choice, choose to sing freely, rejoice in my own sound
Rejoice in the voice I've found.
But sadly, I hear the other voices mock:
"Broken things just can't talk."

Too Quiet

I 've always been told I'm too quiet.
In speaking; in life.
And maybe that's true.
Maybe I'm not meant to rise with the brilliant sun,
maybe I'm meant to bask in dark and shadow.

Maybe I could be the moon, softly glowing from a great distance.
But if I am to be the moon, then she is to be the sun.

She is the most radiant person I've ever met,
positively bursting with life.
She shines like the sun itself,
warming you from the outside in.
She is the dawn you eagerly await with bated breath.

Much like the sun, I feel like I could be burned if I get too close or stare too
long.
But everything about her draws you in,
her exuberant laughter
her unabashed full smile.

She is sunshine itself.
  Sunshine personified
  sunshine identified.
  She is the long-awaited summer after a harsh, frigid winter.
  She is the season you long for.

But the absolute most breathtakingly beautiful thing about her?
  Her voice.

Her voice is a symphony.
  Captivating
  enthralling
  she speaks, and you listen.

She wouldn't be silenced like so many women are.
  And so, so many women are.
  Told they're too loud,
  too boisterous,
  too much.
  They try to silence us with these worded weapons
  like they silenced me.

But not her. She would clutch onto her voice even if it killed her.
  Claws dug in; she wouldn't let them rip it from her.
  It was hers and no one else's,
  and they'd have to pry her cold, dead fingers from her corpse before she
gave away the precious voice she held.

Girl.
  You are the perfect pitch,
  the perfect volume,
  the perfect sound.

I've always been told I'm too quiet. In speaking; in life.
    And I know that's true.
    I've been silenced and shamed for it.
    Silenced and praised for it.

I'm not meant to rise with the brilliant sun,
    I'm meant to bask in dark and shadow.
    I am the moon, softly glowing from a great distance.
    But if I am to be the moon, then you ARE the sun.
    And the burning sun never let anyone keep her from shining.

Stay Silent

Sometimes, I know my thoughts are unhinged,
so silence becomes a second skin.
Something else to wear when I have weird things to share.
Much better to stay quiet despite the riot in my mind,
leave those thoughts behind
closed doors.
It's not as if I'm heard anyway,
so it really doesn't matter.
I don't really matter.
I bite tongues when I really want to bite back,
instead, bite back any comeback
I might have had to spit,
sit down instead.
Stay seated. Stay silent.
Wrap the quiet around my shoulders like a heated blanket
blanketed silence a second skin,,
because in silence, I can't say anything you decipher as sin,
can't be forsaken,
words can't be ignored, misunderstood, or mistaken,
no deliberate misinterpretation.
If I stay quiet when I want to respond,

I'll be the only one drowning in my oceanic word pond.
I'll be the only one living in a skin of silence
so natural it blends right in with my epidermis.
Just the right shade, a color match, just the right fit
a comfortable, fashionable quietness.

Derealization

Lately, I don't feel real...
   Like I'm derealizing my consciousness
   An out-of-body experience this
Maybe out-of-mind interference
Because I feel like I'm out of my mind
reactions lagging behind
I can't seem to find myself.
Sleepwalking through my life
Like I'm someone else
And I'm not sure if I want to wake up.
Leave me in this fever dream
Where nothing seems real
And I don't have to feel anymore.
Dissociate, disconnect, deflect, distance, dissonance
No resistance
Let my mind take me away, far away
Lost in my mind,
A foggy haze
Lost in my mind,
A foggy daze
Lost in my mind

For days.
Please don't wake me
Please don't make me
Deal with these realities
Let me live in waking dreams
In walking fantasies
Where daydreaming can't be as bad as living seems.

Face Eulogy

F ace ~~Eu~~
     Apology:

    I need to write an apology to my face—face it:
This is more of an eulogy.
I have had your funeral a thousand times; I've just never apologized for it.
But I sure did bury you in thick, pale ivory makeup,

Throwing dirt on the coffin.

I hate my face—rephrase—I hate the brown birthmark marring my right
cheek.

Which is half my face,
   So, I
   Half-hate it,
   I
   Have-hated it,
   I

Have been told I'm brave when I don't wear makeup.

A new meaning for "putting On a brave face."
    Only,
    I'm not putting it "On"—it's already "On."
    It's my skin that's "On," and praising me for wearing MY skin is a slap On the face.
    Stop kicking the dead horse, there is nothing here for you to ride in On.

No, it's not dirt or chocolate or a bruise or smeared foundation.
    NO, you cannot touch it.

Eyes stray; stay focused on my face.
    The entitlement is abhorrent. Strangers have grabbed my face, asking what's on it,
    Saying they wanted to fix it—"fix your face, girl, I just didn't want you to walk around like that."

I've been walking around like this my entire life.

But I've stopped. Now, I won't go out without covering it with cover-up, cover girl, cover it up, girl.

I don't wear foundation to feel pretty. I wear concealer to conceal,
    Blend in—brush in—bronze in—blush in
    Bury brown birthmark, unmarked grave.

And just everyone has an opinion on girls wearing makeup—shut up.
    This is MY eulogy.
    No.
    This is my…

Face Apology:

I am so sorry for letting questions, comments, touches, and insults bury you.

The "pretty *ifs.*"
"She would be pretty *if* she didn't have the ugly birthmark."

I'm sorry that it hurt me enough to hide you.
I'm sorry that it still hurts enough to keep hiding you.

But.
I know,
You are not an undisturbed grave.
And I can still raise you from the dead.

Sorry I'm Sorry

We all have a friend who berates us for apologizing—no gentleness,
        just a seatbelt lock jarring stop.
        I'm sorry—shit—I said it again,
how do I begin
to explain,
I swear that I'm sane,
it's just something my brain
was trained to do,
and if that doesn't make sense to you,
it will in due time,
I do time in this prison cell,
my personal hell of apologies.
It's appalling me,
stalling me in the middle of traffic,
my mind wreaking havoc,
a collision without my permission,
precision of my condition,
conditioned to say: "Hey. I'm sorry."
It's just another motor accident,
don't leave a dent,
I've got the best intent to hit the brakes,

cuz I know you want me to stop like this sign,
you sigh— say, "Stop saying sorry, don't apologize."
You hypothesize
that I'll be free to just be me, unapologetically— and I know you mean well
but I'm here to tell you —hear my inflection—
I'm sliding through this intersection,
an inspection reflection introspection on the infection of my recollection
of self-protection—
shows a coping mechanism,
mechanic deflection.
Like an airbag to stop whiplashing,
face-bashing,
clashing with the steering wheel, leaving less to heal,
after all,
who would feel
like hitting someone who's sorry?
It's the cushion I leave to fall on,
curl up in a ball on,
with no one to call on,
I'm sorry.
I can't break this habit,
I'm sorry.
I just can't have it,
when you grow up with abuse,
there are things that you just get used to,
I'm sorry.
My muscle memory grabs that clutch,
my crutch to stop before I collide,
a knee-jerk reaction inside,
I'm sorry.
There's a red light in the middle of this road,
and I fight to get out of this fight-or-flight mode,
but there's no magic code

to shut off my sorries,

I'm on sorry overload,

and I know you told me to be more like Demi or Beyoncé: Sorry, NOT sorry,

But I AM sorry—

I am so, so sorry—

I'm sorry THAT I'm sorry.

But being berated is what created my apologies in the first place,

so please, slow down.

Go with the pace of traffic.

Because in my experience,

honking my horn has never made the person in front of me go any faster,

just created more sorry disasters.

Madness

Have you ever felt like you're on the edge of a cliff?
Like a rift
in time could send you over?
On the precipice of something dangerous
One step and you'll plunge
Into the abyss
Sanity, something amiss
I'd be remiss
If I didn't kiss clarity goodbye
A gentle kiss
A gentle lie
How could you watch me cry?
How could you watch me die?
I pry a sigh from cracked and bloodied lips
My mind slips
The deepest sadness
Teetering on the edge of madness

Darker Prayer

Now I lay me down to die
    Let me lie
      And pray my soul
Not be left high and dry
Darker themes
And screaming cries
Pretty prayers
For ugly lives.
Morning in mourning
Before still eyes
See morning light
As last breath dies.
Keep my soul
Or throw it out
But know; I know
Without a doubt
Of pretty soul
I'm found wanting
Of ugly soul
Heavens scream and shout.
I'm not meant

For pretty clouds
For soft wings
And halo crowns
Only darkened shrouds
And blackened roses
Golden gate slams and closes
An iron clank ringing
Off to the fires
No angels singing
Off to the pits
Of hell and burning
Eternal fire licking
Away flesh and bone
I've come to accept
Shuddering and alone
Hell is all I've ever known.

Bruised Kindness

My mind is a map of bruised kindness.
Thoughts I've beaten into myself
over and over,
leaving mark after mark.
Because self-mutilation
is easier than other's humiliation.
Self-manipulation
to meet my "kindness" expectation.
I have no other explanation
as to why my brain is black and blue,
battered into a green-bruised hue.
But sadly, all the violence in the world…
couldn't instill self-kindness.

Carving Kindness

I want to be more kind,
    kind and compassionate,
    compassionately empathetic,
empathetically nice.
I might need advice,
because what I've been doing so far
is hardly working.
I've been carving.
Carving kindness into my bones
with a pointed dagger,
dagger sharpened to a point,
pointless, futile scraping over bone.
It's hard work hacking into ivory.
I seem to be under the impression
if I replace bone marrow with compassion,
maybe I'll be made of the stuff.
This is flawed logic,
logically, I know this.
Hurting myself doesn't help others.
Mutilating bones can never transform me,
never let me embody the kindness I want to see.

Carving kindness won't work with even the sharpest knife
if I'm not even kind with my own life.

Mind Minefield

M y thoughts are attacking me today…
Like mental explosions and imaginary implosions,
thought-bombs and shrapnel-showers
tearing apart my mental state.
It's amazing, the mind's powers as it devours me whole.
But the attack is so pointed; direct.
Shredding me by revealing intimate flaws, a lawless atrocity.
Pulling a knife on my anxiety, my sadness, my pathetic self-esteem,
every thought I have toward myself so mean.
This attack… feels personal.

I've been in survival mode so long,
I've forgotten how to do thrival mode.
More importantly, I've forgotten kindness mode.
Specifically self-kindness, instead of mindless mental self-harm.
It's alarming how bad I've let it get.
How dangerous, how violent, my harmful mindset.
I know I'm hurting myself.
A mental minefield I'm not even trying to navigate.
Not even trying to avoid.
Not even trying to negate my mind's void.

It's like I've given up the battle

and I wish each thought-explosion wouldn't rattle my soul.

My thoughts are attacking me today, but I wish it wouldn't run away with me.

Pointing out the flaws of my personality.

This feels personal.

Like I can't get the violence out of my skull,

can't separate the logic from the emotional.

Yeah, my thoughts are attacking me.

And I'm putting up a poor defense.

Breakable

Do not hold me like I am already broken
  but please
  hold me like I'm breakable.
Fragile.
Like something precious to protect.
Something to gently cup with both hands.
Please don't expect
invincibility.

Call me softly,
  with gentle voice,
  like my name is the softest thing to pass your lips,
  a gentle kiss.
  Call me softly,
  call me sweetly,
  call me sweetie.
  Please.
  Hear my plea.

I crave gentleness
  like the strongest drug,

addicted to softness
like I don't know where I'll find my next hit,
fucking desperate for it.

Don't hold me like I'm broken,
    even though I feel like I am.
    Hold on, embrace me wholly and tenderly,
    like you might be
    the one to finally shatter me.
    Because, honestly,
    I think you just might be.

Blue is My Bias

Blue is my bias,
      and by this,
         I mean a breath of blue.
   Blue reminds me of air.
   Of skies, of calm, of fair.

Blue is my bias,
   and by this,
      I mean blue-stare, we share locked gaze in a haze; this craze is just a phase.

When I told you that you didn't even know my favorite color,
   I meant you didn't know my favorite feature.
   You said you "think it's pink."
   You think.
   I know.

Blue is my bias,
   and by this,
      I mean, blue is my favorite feature.

When I look in the mirror,
   And all I hear are
my own self-criticisms,
I think back to air.
To skies, calm, fair—my eyes.
The blue that inks my eyes.
The only thing I don't despise about myself, despite myself.

Blue is my bias,
   and yes, I'm biased,
But I had to try this.
To pick just *one* thing not to hate about myself.

And if blue represents calm,
   then I want to look myself in the eyes to find that oasis in my own gazes,
and maybe that's vain, yes.
Jealous of everyone around me I see,
   But today, I don't choose green envy, I mean, envy green, I mean, I choose
me.

Air, skies, calm, fair, eyes.
   I choose blue.

Because blue is my bias.

Acknowledgments

I'd like to first thank my boyfriend, David, for always loving me unconditionally and being there for me. You push me to keep going, even when I want to quit. He also hypes up all of my creative projects, even when I get shy about them. I love you so much—you're the bee's knees!

Thank you so much to my primordial ooze twin for her beautiful cover art and the ever-aggressive love and support. Shelby aka "Ari" aka "@inkingteatroll" is my ride-or-die and designated extrovert <3 We're going to have so much fun in June!

Thank you to my friend Dani for reminding me to have grace for myself, pushing me to keep going, and always giving me so much encouragement. She is one of the kindest people I know.

Thank you to Doraly for not only encouraging me and complimenting me, but letting me borrow her as a soundboard <3 And letting me use one of our collaborations! She's an amazing friend, poet, and beta reader!

Thank you to my friend Sammy for loving my poetry and always supporting me no matter what! She's a gem <3

Thank you to my high school speech coach, Gayle, for helping me find my voice in interpretation, and for supporting me through the years.

Thank you to my college speech and debate coach, Amorette, for getting me into Spoken Word in the first place. Her encouragement and coaching have impacted me more than I can ever say. She's one of my OG poetry supporters, and I'm so thankful for her.

Thank you to my Instagram poetry community; there are way too many to list! Lilith for letting me complain about everything writing <3 Helen for always giving me such positive energy and genuine enthusiasm and giving me confidence in Spoken Word. Phoenix for always hyping me up and complimenting my work. Eric for creating dope collabs with me. Sir Von Doom for letting me ask endless publishing questions. And all of the poets who do prompts on their pages that get me in a creative space.

Thank you to both my family and David's family <3 Jasmine for always letting me run poems by her and always understanding the emotion behind it.

I'd like to thank Poetry Nation and Eber & Wein Publishing for including one of the poems in this book in their Anthology, "Figments of the Heart." They included my poem, "Anger is Easier Than Sadness."

And a seemingly random thank you to the band Stray Kids for inspiring me with their music and generally chaotic nature—143 <3 (No, I do not personally know any of them, I just really like to write while their music is playing).

Finally, thank you so much to everyone who read my book! I appreciate you all :)

About the Author

Kristen writes both poetry and fiction. She lives with her boyfriend David, cat Khaleesi, and tortoise Grogu. She is an enthusiastic Stay with an Etsy dedicated to making fan bracelets and an accidental fan TikTok (it's complicated). Kristen is a freelance editor on Fiverr and has a poetry Instagram under: @kristenjewel_writing. She plans to release her first fiction novel in the near future, so stay tuned for news!

You can connect with me on:

- https://www.kristenjewel-writing.com
- https://www.instagram.com/kristenjewel_writing
- https://www.fiverr.com/kristenjewel?public_mode=true
- https://stayvilla.etsy.com

9 798992 132304